A SIGN

A SIGN

story by **George Ella Lyon** pictures by **Chris K. Soentpiet**

ORCHARD BOOKS • NEW YORK

When I was a little girl
our neighbor, Leon Lasseter,
made neon signs.

I loved those bright outlines
of a cup of coffee, a car.
I thought they were Leon signs.

And when I grew up
I wanted to make them too.

My daddy's dry cleaners
had its own neon sign
hung just outside
a second-story window.

NU-WAY, it said,
each letter buzzing, beautiful.

Once Daddy drove me
around a mountain to Virginia
just to see a florist's
neon rose.

When I was a little older
my mother took me to the circus
across the mountain in Tennessee.

I sat by the elephants
and watched a tightrope walker
work the silver line.

So high
          so strong
                    each step
                              her life
in the balance.

"That's for me," I said.

Back home, I put on my swimsuit—
no sequins, not even a ruffle—
and got my red umbrella.

After a few practice trips
out an elm branch and back,
I walked Mrs. Haygood's clothesline.

Sky for my tent, a circus girl, a wonder.
I didn't fall at all

until the clothesline broke.

When I was just enough older
to know about outer space,
Alan Shepard was set
to go up in a rocket.

The school got a TV
so all of us could watch
its roar and fire and smoke
and white plumes climbing.

He was leaving earth behind,
writing a road to the stars.
That's what I wanted to do.

I'd build a rocket in the backyard
and send it straight to the moon.

I wrote to the President:

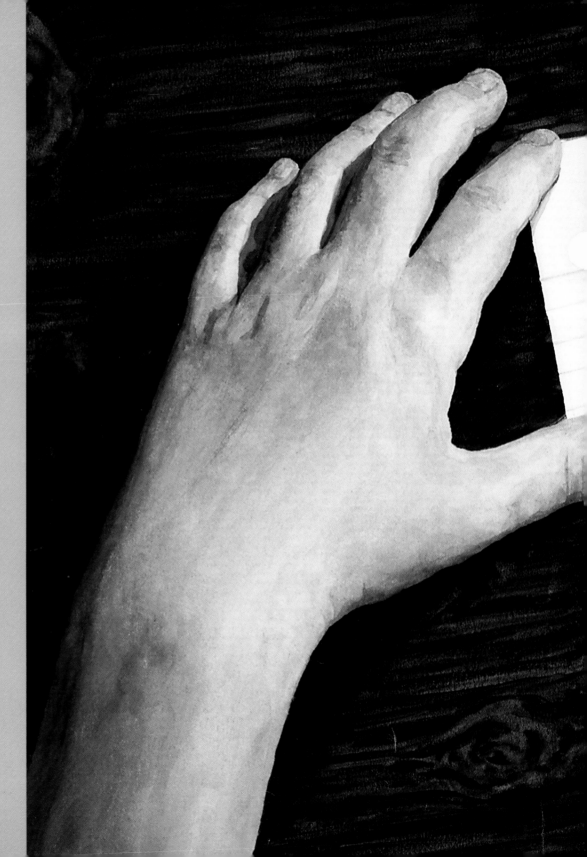

Dear President Kennedy,

Do I have to come to Cape Canaveral or can I launch it right here at Baxter? If my cat Patches wont go can I ride in the rocket myself?

Now that I am grown
I don't bend glass tubes with fire
like Leon Lasseter did

but I try to make words glow.

I don't work the high wire
fifty feet above your head.

I put one word
                 in front
                          of the other
here at my desk
and hope the story won't fall.

And as for that rocket
blasting out into space
headed for the moon

it's your heart I send these words to.
They light the dark between us.

A sign.

In thanksgiving for my parents,
GLADYS and ROBERT HOSKINS,
who nurtured my dream.
—G.E.L.

For MOM,
who influenced me to take all those
art classes outside of high school.
I love you.
—C.K.S.

Text copyright © 1998 by George Ella Lyon. Illustrations copyright © 1998 by Chris K. Soentpiet. All rights reserved. No part of this book may be reproduced or transmitted in any form or by any means, electronic or mechanical, including photocopying, recording or by any information storage or retrieval system, without permission in writing from the Publisher. Orchard Books, 95 Madison Avenue, New York, NY 10016. Manufactured in the United States of America. Printed by Barton Press, Inc. Bound by Horowitz/Rae. The text of this book is set in 18 pt. Goudy Sans Medium. The illustrations are watercolor paintings reproduced in full color.   10 9 8 7 6 5 4 3 2 1
Library of Congress Cataloging-in-Publication Data. Lyon, George Ella, date. A sign / by George Ella Lyon ; illustrated by Chris K. Soentpiet.   p.   cm.   Summary: The author simply describes how she considered various careers as she grew and how she combined them all into her work as a writer. ISBN 0-531-30073-0 (trade : alk. paper) —ISBN 0-531-33073-7 (lib. bdg. : alk. paper) 1. Lyon, George Ella, date.—Biography—Juvenile literature. 2. Women authors, American—20th century—Biography—Juvenile literature. 3. Children's literature—Authorship—Juvenile literature. 4. Lyon, George Ella, date. [1. Authors, American. 2. Women—Biography.] I. Soentpiet, Chris K., ill. II. Title. PS3562. Y4454Z467 1998 813'.54—dc21 [B] 97-26878